"'Twas midnight on the ocean,
Not a streetcar was in sight;
The sun was shining brightly,
For it rained all day that night.
'Twas a summer day in winter
And snow was raining fast,
As a barefoot boy with shoes on
Stood sitting in the grass."

Weather Station

How does a TV weather reporter know what the weather will be like? Let's take a field trip to find out.

As your bus pulls up in front of a TV weather station, the air becomes windy and cloudy. You run for the front door as the first drops of rain fall. The weather reporter greets you at the door. The reporter begins to tell you how the station gathers weather news.

The weather reporter gathers facts about weather from many instruments on the roof and inside the station. A satellite dish collects signals from weather satellites. Computers help the weather reporter understand local and worldwide weather.

- Where does the water come from when it rains?
- Why does the wind blow?
- What is the weather like in January where you live?

Unit D

WATER & WEATHER

Activities

Features

Chapter 1

Water

Do you ever think about water? Most of the earth is covered with water. Where is much of this water stored? Most people just use water and don't wonder where it comes from. When you're thirsty, you may think about clean, fresh water. When someone hands you a glass of water, you're glad to see it.

You almost got soaked in that sudden rainstorm at the weather station. You weren't very glad to see that water! You should have checked the weather report this morning. Then you would have known that you needed an umbrella. Weather reports are done by **meteorologists** (mēt′ē ər äl′ə jists), scientists who study weather.

Meteorologists make weather predictions. They predict when rain will fall in your area. They predict if where you live is going into a dry time or a wet one.

SCIENCE JOURNAL

Knowing if there is going to be enough rainfall is important because people use water in many ways. In your Science Journal, list all the ways you can think of that people use water.

A rain gauge measures the amount of rainfall.

Explore Activity

How can you make water appear?

Process Skills
Observing, Inferring, Hypothesizing

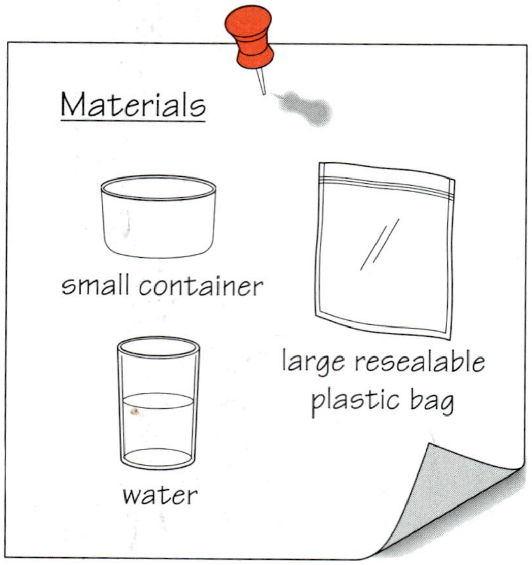

Observe and Collect Data

1. Fill the small container about one-quarter full with water.
2. Place the container inside the plastic bag. Seal the bag.
3. Find a sunny spot and place the bag there. When you pick up the bag to move it to a sunny spot, be sure to hold onto the container full of water. This will keep the container from tipping over and spilling the water.
4. ACTIVITY JOURNAL Go back and look at the bag after 30 minutes. Touch the bag to see if it is hot or cold, or moist or dry. In your Activity Journal, record your observations.

Share Your Results

1. What do you think happened in the bag?
2. Did other classmates make the same observations as you? Explain your answer.

Draw Conclusions

1. How did the bag feel?
2. Where did the water on the inside of the bag come from?

Apply What You Know

Look around your home and school. Where else have you seen water droplets collecting or falling like those you observed here?

Where is fresh water found on the earth?

Most of the water on our planet is found in the great huge oceans. Can you drink the water from the ocean? Can you water a plant with salty water from the ocean? Most animals and plants that live on land need fresh water.

In some places, there is plenty of fresh water. In other places, there is little. Even in places that have plenty of fresh water, only part of that water is on the earth's surface.

Some fresh water is found underground. It is called **ground water.** To use ground water, people drill wells and pump the water to the surface.

An iceberg is a huge chunk of ice that floats in the ocean.

In some places, ground water comes to the surface of the earth to form a spring. Spring water flows out onto the surface.

Another source of the earth's fresh water is ice. This ice is found in places where it is always cold. It is found on the tops of high mountains or near the North and South Poles.

Ground water is below the earth's surface.

This pond is in Yosemite National Park in California. Rainwater, melted snow, or ground water have filled up the pond. Plants and animals found near here need and use this fresh water.

Be a Scientist

HANDS-ON ACTIVITY

What makes ice melt?

1. Put an ice cube in each of two shallow dishes. Place one dish in a shaded area and one dish in sunlight or under a bright lamp. Time how long it takes each ice cube to melt.
2. Now hold an ice cube in your hand. How fast does it melt? How does the ice cube make your hand feel? What is needed to make ice melt?

How does water enter the air?

Did you ever wonder where water goes when something wet dries? The water changes into an invisible gas called water vapor. The water vapor goes into the air. This change is called **evaporation** (ē vap′ə rā′shən).

Even though you cannot see it or smell it, there is almost always some water vapor in the air. The amount of water vapor in the air is called **humidity.** How much water vapor the air can hold depends on how warm the air is. Warm air holds more water vapor than cold air. On hot summer days, the air can feel sticky. This is because the warm air holds a large amount of water vapor. The humidity is high.

Amazing!

Did you know that you add water vapor to the air? Each time you breathe out, you give off water vapor and a gas called carbon dioxide. Animals also give off water vapor when they breathe.

Water evaporates from oceans, lakes, rivers, and plants.

▶ Compare the trees of the Merchants Millpond State Park in North Carolina with the cactus of Arizona you see here. Both swampy and desert areas that you see can have very warm air. Why do you think the park in North Carolina is more humid than the desert of Arizona?

How does water leave the air?

This man takes care of all the weather equipment for the TV station. He tests the instruments on the roof and the other weather equipment in the building.

Have you ever come out of a shower to find the bathroom mirror "fogged up"? The hot shower water adds water vapor to the bathroom air. This moist air strikes the cool mirror. Some of the water vapor in the air changes into water droplets. The change from water vapor to water is called **condensation** (kän′dən sā′shən). Tiny droplets of water collect on the mirror.

In the Explore Activity, water condensed on the inside of the plastic bag. Water vapor in the air changed into water droplets. On a clear morning, have you ever noticed tiny water droplets on the grass? At night, the air is warmer than the grass. Water vapor in the air condenses, and water collects on the grass.

Water vapor in the air condenses, forming clouds.

It's raining on the ocean! Tiny water droplets of a cloud join together and form larger drops. The drops get so heavy, they fall from the clouds as rain.

SCIENCE JOURNAL

Make a list of things around your home that change when humidity changes. Look for things that happen on a warm, wet day when the humidity is high. For example, what things feel wet or slippery? Describe how these things seem different on a cool, dry day when the humidity is low.

BACK HOME

How are you doing?

1. Where is the earth's fresh water found?
2. Why does the air around you sometimes feel sticky?
3. **Think** Compare evaporation and condensation.

What is the water cycle?

Think of all the fresh water that is used every day. Plants take in water from the soil through their roots. Animals drink water. People use water in hundreds of ways. And yet the earth's total supply of fresh water does not change.

With so much water being used, how is this possible? Nature has a way of "recycling" water, or using it over and over. This reusing of water in nature is called the water cycle. You have already seen parts of the water cycle. Find those parts in this drawing.

1. Energy from the sun heats water in oceans, lakes, rivers, and streams. The water evaporates and becomes water vapor that moves into the air.

2. Water vapor rises high into the air. High above the earth's surface, the air cools. Water vapor condenses into tiny water droplets to form clouds.

YOU CAN HELP

SCIENCE JOURNAL

Many businesses that use fresh water clean it and reuse it over and over. List in your Science Journal ways you might reuse water at home or school. Try something from the list.

3. Billions of tiny drops come together to form larger drops of water. When the drops become too heavy, they fall to the earth's surface as rain, snow, or hail.

4. At the surface, some water falls into rivers, lakes, and oceans. Some soaks into the ground. Rivers and ground water flow downhill into oceans or lakes.

In some places water that looks clean isn't clean because people have added harmful things to it. You must be careful not to pollute your water.

How can you save water?

The water cycle happens over and over. But clean, fresh water is not always where people need it. Most water on the earth is in the oceans. This water cannot be used because it is salty. Sometimes not enough rain falls in a place. The water supply can get very low.

Sometimes people waste water. It is important to save water whenever you can. Use only as much water as you really need.

Be a Scientist

HANDS-ON ACTIVITY

How does the earth store water?

1. ACTIVITY JOURNAL Use a dry sponge to represent a rock below the earth's surface. In your Activity Journal, describe the sponge.
2. Place the sponge in a container. Pour water over the sponge until all of it is wet.
3. Stand the sponge on end. Add two drops of food coloring to the top of the wet sponge. Describe what happens. Imagine that the sponge stores ground water. How does ground water become polluted? How can you keep ground water clean?

Ways to Conserve Water

Things you can do at home and at school	Amount of water saved
Fill the bathtub halfway instead of full.	68 liters
Sweep sidewalks instead of hosing them down.	38 liters per minute
Put trash in a wastebasket, not down the toilet.	19 liters per minute
Do not let the water run when you brush your teeth.	19 liters

Look at the table for ways to save water. When you use fresh water, it may not be safe for anyone else to use right away. After water goes down the drain, it has to be recycled.

How are you doing?

1. What happens to water vapor when it gets high above the ground?
2. What are two ways that fresh water can be wasted?
3. **Think** Give three examples of water moving from the earth's surface to the air in the water cycle.

Science & Literature Connection

STORM IN THE NIGHT

WRITTEN BY MARY STOLZ
ILLUSTRATED BY PAT CUMMINGS

Grandfather tells Thomas a story about when he was a boy. And in case you're wondering, Melvin was grandfather's dog.

". . . Melvin was out on some errand of his own, and I was doing my homework, when all at once, with only a rumble of warning . . .
down came the rain, *down* came the lightning, and all around and everywhere came the thunder."

"Wow," said Thomas. "What did you do?"

"Dove under the bed."

"But what about Melvin?"

"I'm *coming* to that," said Grandfather. "What-about-Melvin is what the story is *about*."

"I see," said Thomas. "This is pretty exciting."

"Well — it was then. Are you going to listen, or keep interrupting?"

"I think I'll listen," said Thomas.

"Good. Where was I?"

"Under the bed."

"So I was. Well, I lay there shivering at every clap of thunder, and I'm ashamed to say that it was some time before I even remembered that my poor little dog was all by himself out in the storm."

Thomas shook his head in the dark.

"And when I did remember," Grandfather went on, "I had the most awful time making myself wriggle out from under the bed and go looking for my father or my mother—to ask them to go out and find Melvin for me."

"Grandfather!"

"I told you I was afraid. This is a true story you're hearing, so I have to tell the truth."

Think About Your Reading

1. How did Grandfather feel about thunderstorms when he was a boy? How can you tell?
2. What do you think happened to Melvin and Grandfather? Finish the story with your own ending.

Communicating Imagine that Grandfather is a young boy again. Write a letter to that young boy. Can you convince him not to be afraid of thunderstorms?

Where to Read More

Verna Aardema, *Bringing the Rain to Kapiti Plain* (Dial Books, 1981)
There is a terrible drought in Africa. What can Ki-pat the herdsboy do about it?

Looking Back

Words and Concepts

Fill in the blanks.

1. Most of the earth's water is found ____.
2. The change from water to ____ is called evaporation.
3. Cold air holds ____ water vapor than warm air.
4. The change from water vapor to water is ____.
5. Because fresh water is not always where you need it, it is important to ____ water.
6. ____ is the amount of water vapor in the air.

Applied Thinking Skills

Answer the following questions. You can use words, drawings, and diagrams in your answers.

7. A cycle is something that happens over and over again. Explain how the diagram below shows a cycle.

8. Describe where in the diagram condensation might take place.
9. What role does the sun play in the cycle below?
10. **Your World** Explain why it is important to save water every day, even though most of the earth's surface is covered by water.

Show What You Know

How can you model the water cycle?

Observe and Collect Data

1. Set up a model like you see below. There is about 3 centimeters of colored water in the bottom of the plastic box.
2. Be sure the lamp is not too close to the plastic wrap. A 100-watt bulb can get very hot.
3. ACTIVITY JOURNAL Wait a few minutes and see what happens. In your Activity Journal, describe what you observe.

Draw Conclusions

1. How does your setup model the water cycle?
2. Where did most of the condensation occur? Why did it occur?

Process Skills
Observing, Inferring, Making models

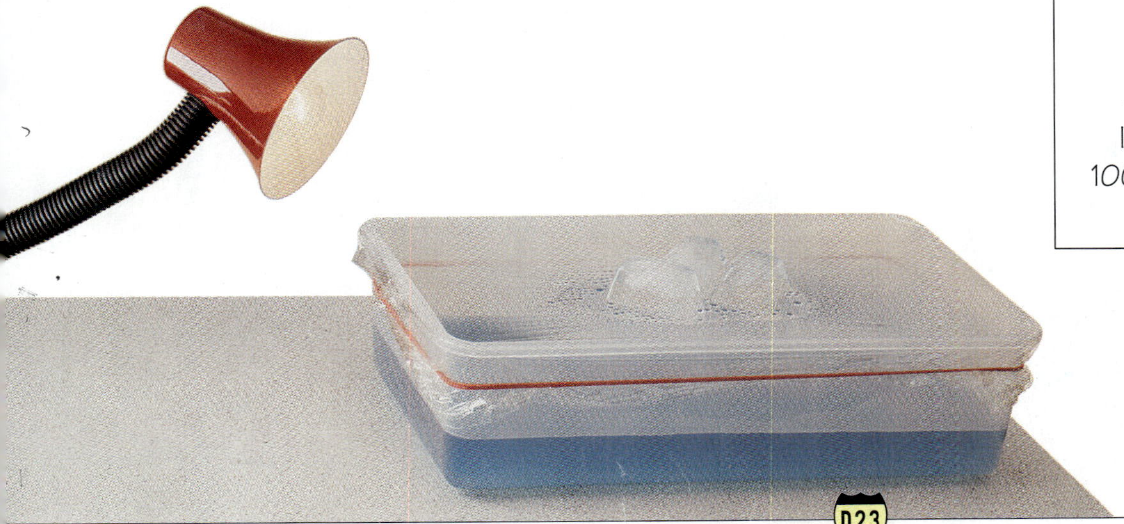

Chapter 2

Weather Conditions

What do you think of when you hear the word "weather"? Most people think about what it's like outside right then. Is it warm or cold? Is it sunny, windy, or rainy? To a meteorologist, **weather** is the state of the air at a certain time and place. The earth is covered with a thick blanket of air. If there were no air, there would be no weather. Almost all weather happens in the layer of air closest to the earth's surface.

Being able to predict, or forecast, the weather is very important. If you know what kind of weather is coming, you can get ready for it. You may need to dress for hot weather or wear a rain slicker. If a storm is coming, you may need to keep out of danger. Weather forecasts help save lives and property.

SCIENCE JOURNAL

Weather is always changing. Weather includes temperature, air pressure, humidity, wind, clouds, and rain or snow. In your Science Journal, describe today's weather.

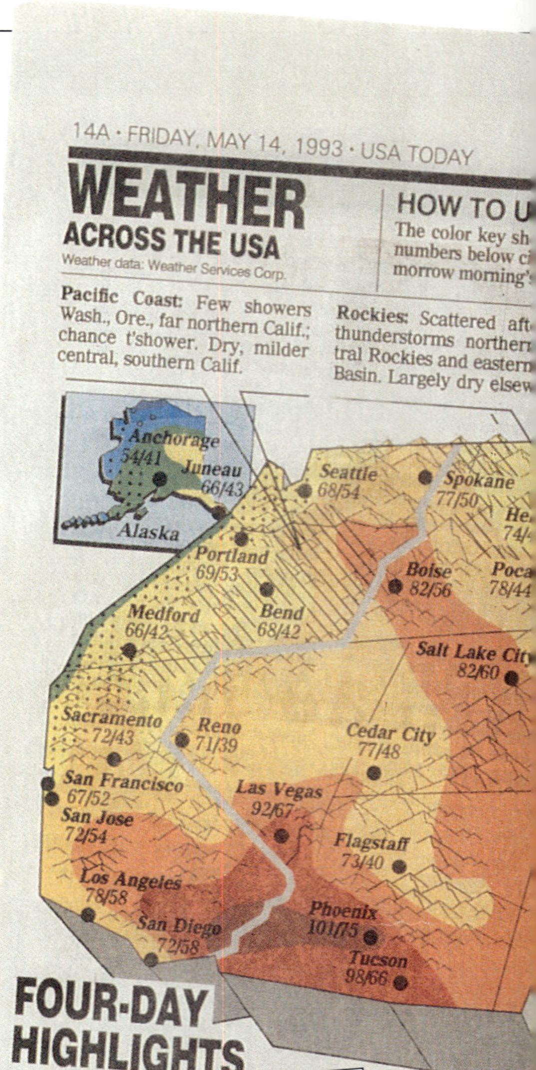

Plenty of sun for the weekend

Sunshine will continue drying out the rain-soaked central USA. But while the weekend will be sunny, no unusually hot weather is expected.

Midwest falling back: It feels like autumn

By Mary Smaragdis
USA TODAY

The calendar says it's spring, but autumnlike conditions will nip the Midwest this weekend.

"A fall-like weather pattern will continue to dominate the Midwest," said Wayne Barnes of Weather Services Corp.

Unseasonably chilly air accompanied by clouds will bring showers and even a chance of May snow to the Midwest and Great Lakes.

This chilly, wet weather will push to the mid-Atlantic and East Coast on Sunday.

... and thunderstorms linger across the Carolinas and Georgia today, but the region will dry out over the weekend.

Wet weather will sweep the Great Plains. Showers and thunderstorms will rumble through the nation's midsection through Sunday.

Dry weather will embrace California and the desert Southwest this weekend.

Temperatures will shoot up to the century mark in the Southwest, while California will see seasonal conditions through Sunday.

Explore Activity

How can you compare temperatures?

Process Skills
Predicting, Measuring, Collecting data

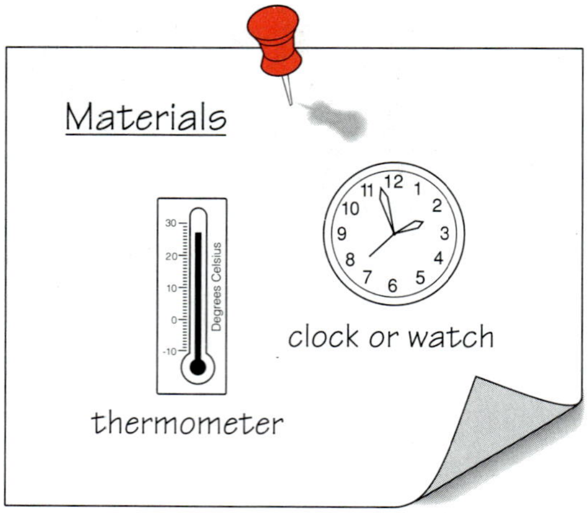

Observe and Collect Data

1. In your Activity Journal, make a data table like the one below. **Predict** and record the room's temperature. Hold a thermometer in the air without touching the bulb for two minutes. Record the air temperature in the data table.
2. Choose one place or item in the room that you **predict** will be cooler than the air you measured. Record the place or item and your prediction. For two minutes, hold the thermometer in that place. Record the temperature.

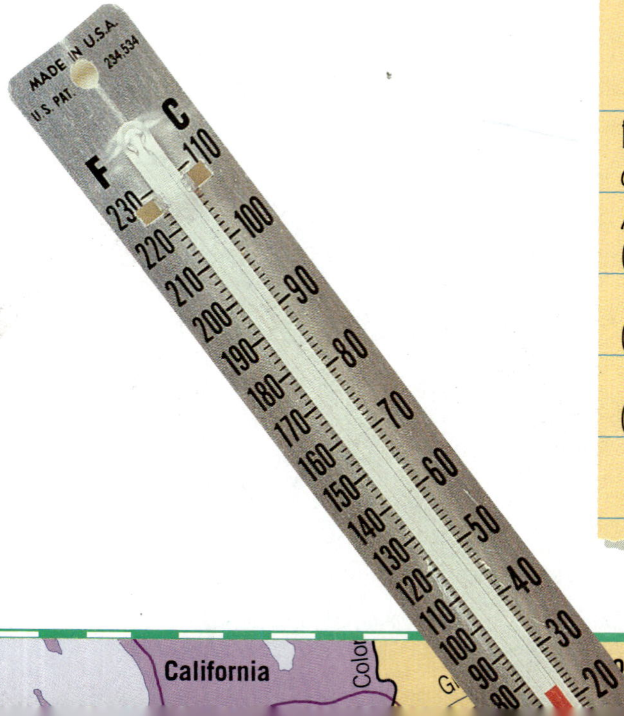

Measuring Temperature

Place or Item	Predicted temperature	Actual temperature	
Air (room temperature)			
(cooler)			
(warmer)			

3. Choose one place or item in the room that you **predict** will be warmer than the air you measured. Record the place or item and your prediction. For two minutes, hold the thermometer in that place. Record its temperature in the data table.

Share Your Results

Compare your results with those of other groups. How many were able to make correct predictions?

Draw Conclusions

1. What places or items were the warmest? What do they have in common?
2. What places or items were the coolest? What do they have in common?

Apply What You Know

What do the results of this activity tell you about temperatures you might measure at home?

Hailstones form when water droplets freeze onto bits of ice. Here you see some huge hailstones that fell on a field outside of Lubbock, Texas.

What is temperature?

All matter is made up of tiny particles. These particles are always moving and have energy. Energy is the ability to make things move or to cause other changes. The more energy the particles have, the faster they move. This causes the matter to get warmer. Temperature is a measure of the amount of energy in something.

Temperature is measured with a thermometer. A thermometer has a temperature scale marked on it. Temperature scales are divided into units called degrees. A small circle (°) is the symbol for degrees.

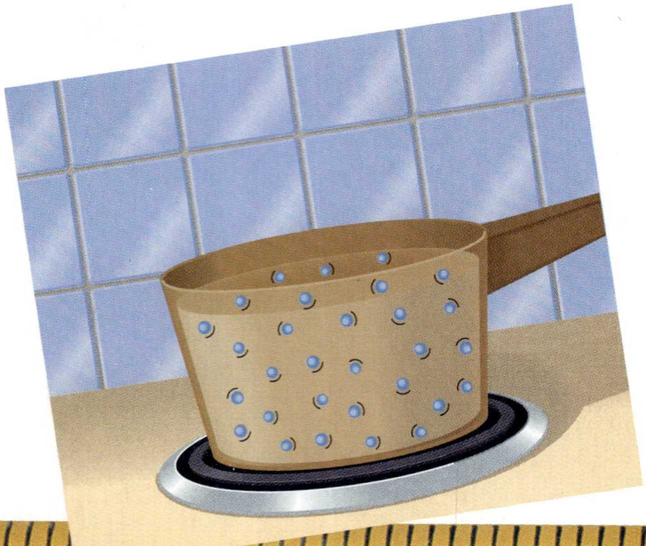

Particles of water move slowly when the water is cold.

Below you see a thermometer with the Celsius temperature scale. The Celsius scale is usually used in science. At 0° Celsius, water freezes. Water boils at 100° Celsius. There is another scale that is commonly used in the United States. It is known as the Fahrenheit scale. The letters *F* and *C* are used as symbols for Fahrenheit and Celsius.

YOU CAN HELP

Some thermometers have a poisonous material called mercury in them. If you break a thermometer and a silvery liquid comes out, ask an adult to help you clean up. Mercury should not be washed down a drain. Ask an adult to find out how to get rid of it.

Particles of water move faster when the water is heated.

Where does the earth's energy come from?

The Egyptians worshipped a sun god named Aton many years ago.The Egyptians carved this stone to honor Aton. Notice how Aton's rays touch and warm even the plants of Egypt.

In the first chapter, you saw that water can change into water vapor. Water vapor can change back into water. When you almost got rained on, you saw how weather can change.

Energy causes changes. For example, the energy of wind can change your umbrella and turn it inside out. The energy in falling rain can flatten small plants. The moving raindrops can force the uplifted plant to one side. All moving things have energy.

There are other kinds of energy, too. Light and heat are kinds of energy. The earth gets heat and light from the sun.

Heat energy causes things to warm up. Heat energy makes water evaporate. You know that the sun feels warm on your skin. Have you ever touched the hood of a car that has been parked in bright sunlight? If so, you know that the metal is hot.

The sun's heat is soaked up by the water tanks, Lexan ceiling, and windows. Lexan gets very hot when the sun's rays strike it. The heat collected here warms the air of this room for a greenhouse.

You might see a layer of white clouds covering part of the earth if you cruised past it in your spacecraft. The rays of the sun shine through a window on your craft. Those same rays shine through the clouds and give heat and light to the blue planet below.

Is the earth heated evenly?

When sunlight strikes matter, some of its energy is absorbed, or taken in, by the matter and changed into heat. This is how the sun heats the earth. Rocks, soil, and water take in energy from the sun and change it into heat. The heat then moves out and warms the air near the earth's surface.

The earth's surface is not the same everywhere. Most of the surface is covered by water. The parts not covered by water are made up of soil, rocks, or ice. Some materials absorb the sun's energy more than others. Soil, rocks, and cement heat up more quickly than water does.

1. Rocks and soil heat up quickly. They absorb more of the sun's energy than does the air or water around them.

2. Like rocks and soil, paved roads heat up quickly.

3. Water in oceans, rivers, and lakes absorbs and loses energy more slowly than nearby land.

Be a Scientist

Do different materials warm up differently?

1. Fill two cups with two different materials. They can include water, dry sand, wet sand, or soil.

2. Place a thermometer in each material. Place both cups about 15 centimeters below a lamp and turn on the lamp. **Predict** which material will become warmer. Do not touch the lamp. Record the temperature and remove the thermometers.

3. In your Activity Journal, record the temperature of each material every 2 minutes for 10 minutes.

4. Which material in the cups warmed up the most? Was your prediction correct?

If you have gone to the beach on a sunny day, you know that the sand gets much hotter than the water. Why is this true?

How are you doing?

1. What are thermometers used for?
2. Why is the surface of the earth heated unevenly?
3. **Think** Why does sunlight feel warm on your skin?

What are air and wind?

You need air to live, but you cannot see it. Clean air has no smell or taste. Air has weight. Although air doesn't weigh much, there is a lot of it. The earth is covered by a layer of air hundreds of kilometers thick. The weight of the air pushing down on the earth's surface is called air pressure.

Air presses against you when it moves. Wind is moving air. Some of the instruments at the weather station measure wind. A **wind vane** shows wind direction. An **anemometer** (an′ə mäm′ət ər) measures wind speed. Weather often changes when the wind changes speed or direction.

Career Corner

Meteorologist

At a TV weather station, my job is to report the weather. My name is Janice Huff, and I am a meteorologist. To decide what the weather will be like, I look at many things. I use weather maps and instruments, satellite photos, computer forecasts, and reports from other meteorologists to help make my predictions. Usually my predictions are correct. Sometimes they are not.

How could air cause pressure? If you were lying in bed under only one bed sheet, you would hardly notice it. You would feel the weight of 1,000 sheets! You and everything on the earth's surface are at the bottom of a layer of air that is something like lying under 1,000 bed sheets. Why do you think you don't feel that pressure?

A wind vane and an anemometer measure the wind's direction and speed.

Windy days are often great days to fly a kite!

Why does wind blow?

Uneven heating of the earth's surface causes wind to blow. A shoreline is a good place to observe the effects of uneven heating.

During the day, land becomes hotter than nearby water. Air over warm land is heated and becomes lighter. This changes its air pressure. Warm air has lower air pressure than cool air.

Air over water during the day is cooler and has higher pressure. Air moves from where pressure is high to where pressure is low. So, cool air over the water moves toward the lower pressure over land. The moving air is wind.

Hot air inside the balloon causes it to rise into the air. Winds carry the floating hot-air balloons from place to place.

Be a Scientist

HANDS-ON ACTIVITY

How can you detect drafts?

1. You can find wind, or a draft, with a simple tool. Cut four strips of tissue, each about 3 centimeters wide. Tape one end of the tissue strips to the end of your pencil.
2. Use your draft detector to check for drafts, or wind, near windows and doors. Check other places where outside air might get into your classroom.
3. Where did you find drafts?

BACK HOME

During cold weather, it is warmer and the air pressure is lower inside a house than outside. Cold air moves into the house through any opening, creating drafts. These drafts waste heat energy. Use your draft detector to find drafts. Ask an adult to help you think of ways to close the openings.

The top picture shows how daytime wind occurs at a shoreline. This wind is called a sea breeze. The bottom picture shows night wind at a shoreline. At night, the land loses heat more quickly than the water. Wind that forms at night is called a land breeze.

What can clouds tell you about the weather?

Clouds are collections of tiny drops of water. Clouds form when water vapor in the air condenses.

There are different types of clouds. You can tell many things about conditions at the earth's surface by studying clouds. As weather in a place changes, the patterns and types of clouds change. These changes give clues about the coming weather.

Cumulus (kyo͞o′myo͞o ləs) **clouds** are white, puffy clouds that look like piles of cotton. They are known as fair-weather clouds because they usually are seen with sunny weather.

Stratus (strāt′əs) **clouds** are gray clouds that cover the lower part of the sky. Rain or snow falls from them.

Cirrus

Cirrus (sir′əs) **clouds** are thin, "feathery" clouds, and they are made of ice crystals. They appear high in the sky. When you see cirrus clouds, it is a sign that rain or snow is on the way.

Cumulonimbus (kyo͞o′ myo͞o lō nim′ bəs) **clouds** are tall, dark clouds that mean thunderstorms with heavy rain and strong winds.

Fog is a cloud that forms at the earth's surface. Fog usually forms when warm, moist air moves over a cold surface, causing water vapor in the air to condense.

How are you doing?

1. What causes wind to blow?
2. What type of clouds usually occur with sunny weather?
3. **Think** At night, land is usually cooler than nearby water. In what direction would you expect the wind to blow? Explain.

VIEWPOINT

You and the Weather

There are many different weather conditions—freezing snow, hot sunshine, wind, and rain are just a few. And there are many feelings people have about the weather.

How might a cold, snowy day make you feel? Some people like the snow. They can ski on it and build snow castles with it. To other people, snow means shoveling the driveway and driving on slippery roads.

How do you feel when there's a thunderstorm on the way? Some people think the loud thunder and bright lightning are fun. To others, it seems scary. It's all a matter of how you look at the weather. You might look at rain as something that traps you inside or keeps your garden from getting too dry.

Data Collection and Analysis

MATH CONNECTION

How can you watch the weather?

Observe and Collect Data

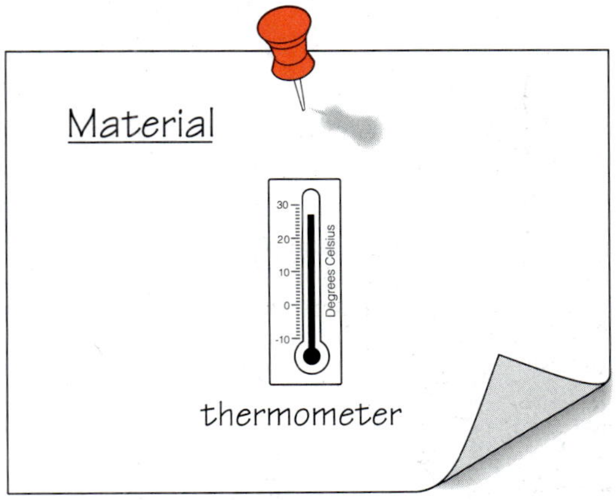

1. Choose some weather conditions to observe over the next five days. For example, you might observe temperature, types of clouds, wind, and amount of sunshine. Keep in mind the equipment or materials you have and can use to make your observations.
2. ACTIVITY JOURNAL In your Activity Journal, create a data table that will help you keep track of the weather conditions you are observing.
3. Over the next five days, observe and record the weather conditions you decided to watch. **Predict** what will happen to the weather conditions you are watching.

Draw Conclusions

Which weather condition(s) that you or your classmates observed changed the most? Were your weather predictions correct? Explain your answer.

Looking Back

Words and Concepts

Choose the best answer to complete the sentence.

1. Temperature, pressure, and humidity are conditions that combine to make ____.

a. clouds **c.** wind
b. weather **d.** air

2. A(n) ____ measures temperature.

a. thermometer **c.** wind vane
b. anemometer **d.** meteorologist

3. Uneven heating of the earth's surface causes ____.

a. snow **c.** pressure
b. humidity **d.** winds

4. A wind vane measures ____.

a. clouds **c.** wind direction
b. fog **d.** heat energy

5. Air usually moves from places of high ____ to low ____.

a. pressure **c.** humidity
b. water vapor **d.** clouds

Applied Thinking Skills

Answer the following questions. You can use words, drawings, and diagrams in your answers.

6. What clouds produce a thunderstorm?

7. Give two examples of why there could be no weather if there were no air.

8. In which would you expect the particles to have more energy, an ice cube or a glass of water? Explain your answer.

9. Explain how fog might form along a river.

10. **Your World** List all the ways you get information about the weather.

Show What You Know

What will your weather be like?

Observe and Collect Data

1. From the radio, television, or newspaper record a three- or five-day weather forecast.
2. ACTIVITY JOURNAL Observe the weather and measure the temperature for the next three to five days. Record the data in your Activity Journal.

Process Skills
Inferring, Measuring, Collecting data

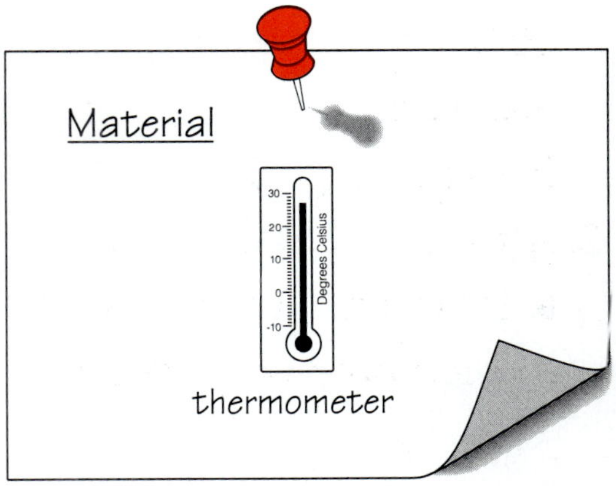

Draw Conclusions

1. How did the weather forecast compare with your observations and measurements?
2. Do you think that predicting the weather is easy or hard? Explain your answer.

Chapter 3

Weather & Climate

When you arrived at the weather station, the weather changed from sunny to rainy. The weather reporter tells you that it is not raining all over your state. Different parts of the same state are having different kinds of weather.

The storm at the weather station is an example of local weather. Local weather is the weather that affects a certain place.

Local weather depends on many things, such as the time of year. Today's rainstorm may be the start of your area's rainy season, which may last a long time. Or it may be due to a change in the air near your town. The rainstorm may not last more than a day.

SCIENCE JOURNAL The pictures on these pages show things that you might use in different kinds of local weather. In your Science Journal, describe today's local weather. Then list those things shown that you might use in weather like you have today.

Explore Activity

How can you tell one season from another?

MINDS-ON ACTIVITY

Process Skills

Observing, Inferring

Observe and Collect Data

Study the pictures. Notice the season in which each picture was taken.

Share Your Results

1. Which location, or place, has the greatest weather changes from season to season?
2. How many classmates agree with your answer to question 1?

Here is Binney Park in Greenwich, Connecticut. It is summertime.

In winter, Binney Park is covered with ice and crunchy snow.

Draw Conclusions

1. Do you think the seasons in these areas are similar from year to year? Why or why not?
2. What kinds of weather changes might occur in these areas from day to day?

Apply What You Know

1. Which location is more like where you live?
2. What kind of weather do you have in the summer and the winter? Draw pictures of winter and summer where you live.

In the summer, fog rolls in around the Golden Gate Bridge in California.

The water of the San Francisco Bay crashes against the shore. It is winter.

How does local weather change?

Your local weather is the weather where you live. How has your local weather changed in the past few days? Think about what it was like yesterday and the day before.

A meteorologist studies air masses when predicting weather. Air masses form at the earth's surface. An air mass that forms over warm, dry land tends to be warm and dry. An air mass that forms over cold water tends to be cold and moist.

Weather changes as one air mass leaves your area and another moves in. Sometimes an air mass slows, or even stops moving. When this happens, the local weather stays the same for several days.

Some weather changes take place over a longer time. The changes shown on pages D46 and D47 are seasonal changes. How are daily weather conditions where you live different in January from July?

When a new air mass moves into an area, it causes the weather to change. A complete weather change usually takes two or three days.

Be a Scientist

What can you learn from a weather map?

Weather can move in many directions. It often moves across the United States from the Pacific Ocean to the Atlantic.

1. ACTIVITY JOURNAL Here is a weather map. Look at the red dot on the map. Imagine that you are standing in the mountains at that point. The map shows a storm in the mountains. In your Activity Journal, describe the weather around you.
2. Over the next few days the storm in the mountains will move.
3. Trace the map you see here in your journal. **Predict** where you think the storm will move in two days. Record your prediction on your map. Where will the storm be the day after that?

Tornados form when a thunderstorm meets strong winds high in the air. The winds cause the storm to spin.

A hurricane off the coast of Palm Beach, Florida, caused these huge waves to form.

What are storms?

There are many different kinds of storms. They all have low air pressure and strong winds.

The most common kind of storm is a thunderstorm. A thunderstorm is a storm with high clouds, heavy rain, strong winds, thunder, and lightning. Some thunderstorms also drop chunks of ice called hail.

A tornado (tôr nā′dō) is the smallest kind of storm, but it can be the most dangerous. A tornado is a funnel-shaped cloud that spins around. From a distance, tornados appear small. But they can have very strong winds that can cause great damage.

Hurricanes (her′i kānz′) are large and powerful storms. They have heavy rains and strong winds. In different parts of the world, these storms are called by other names, such as typhoons.

As a hurricane moves over warm ocean waters, it gets bigger and stronger. Its strong winds can push huge ocean waves on shore. The waves and heavy rains can cause floods. The winds can also blow down trees and destroy buildings.

The Barometer

A barometer (bə räm′ət ər) is used to measure air pressure. One kind of barometer is the mercury barometer. Changes in air pressure are shown on it by the mercury in a glass tube going up and down. The mercury barometer you see below was made and used nearly 300 years ago. Another type of barometer is the aneroid (an′ər oid′) barometer. When air pressure changes, the pointer moves along a scale. Today most meteorologists use computers to keep track of local air pressure. They also look at humidity, rainfall, winds, and temperature to help make their weather predictions.

Using barometers, meteorologists can closely watch air pressure. A change in air pressure usually means that the weather will soon change. The air pressure change may mean a storm is on the way. Air pressure usually drops when a storm is coming.

computer

aneroid barometer

mercury barometer

What are some unusual weather conditions?

On your tour of the weather station you noticed it was still raining. Imagine that it rained for one whole week after that. In your Science Journal, describe what would happen if it rained continuously for one week.

If water overflows into an area in a short time, a flood may occur. A flood can be caused by a large amount of rainfall.

Some floods are effected by warm weather. Sudden warm weather in early spring can cause winter snow and ice to melt quickly. The extra water flows into rivers, and the rivers overflow their banks.

Swiftly flowing floodwaters can destroy homes and drown people and animals. Floods can also destroy crops and wash away valuable soil.

Sometimes, the weather in an area does not change for a long time. When this happens, life in the area is affected. If a place does not get rain for a long period, there is a drought (drout). If the drought lasts a long time, plants and animals may die.

Not much can be done to control weather that produces droughts and floods. In some places, dams have been built to control flooding. These dams also hold some of the water and save it for use when it is needed.

HANDS-ON ACTIVITY

What absorbs water?

1. Pour water into a cup until the water level is 6 centimeters high. Add some cotton balls to the water. When they are completely wet, remove them with a spoon.

2. Measure the level of the water. If the water level is lower, the cotton balls absorbed some of the water.

3. Repeat this experiment with two other materials given to you by your teacher. Which materials absorbed water?

Normally rain absorbs into the soil. At times it rains so hard that the soil can't absorb the rain. In the summer of 1993, heavy rains near the Mississippi River flooded places like this stadium in Iowa.

How are you doing?

1. What two things do all storms have in common?
2. What is a drought?
3. **Think** An air mass over your area has slowed down and stopped moving. What might your weather be like over the next few days?

What is climate?

Suppose someone asked you what the weather is like where you live. How would you answer? What does that person really want to know about your weather? He or she probably wants to know what the climate, rather than the weather, is like where you live. **Climate** describes the weather of a place over a long time.

The two most important parts of climate are the temperature and the amount of rain or snow. Some parts of Ethiopia are warm most of the time. Some places, like Antarctica, are cold all year.

In some places, the weather changes during the year. Such places have cool winters and warm summers. In southern Florida and southern California, the temperature difference between summer and winter is not very great. But in Minnesota and Connecticut there is a big temperature difference between summer and winter.

Most places get enough, but not too much, rain or snow throughout the year. Others have seasons with a lot of rain or snow or with none at all. In India, for example, most of the rain falls during the summer, and very little will fall during the rest of the year.

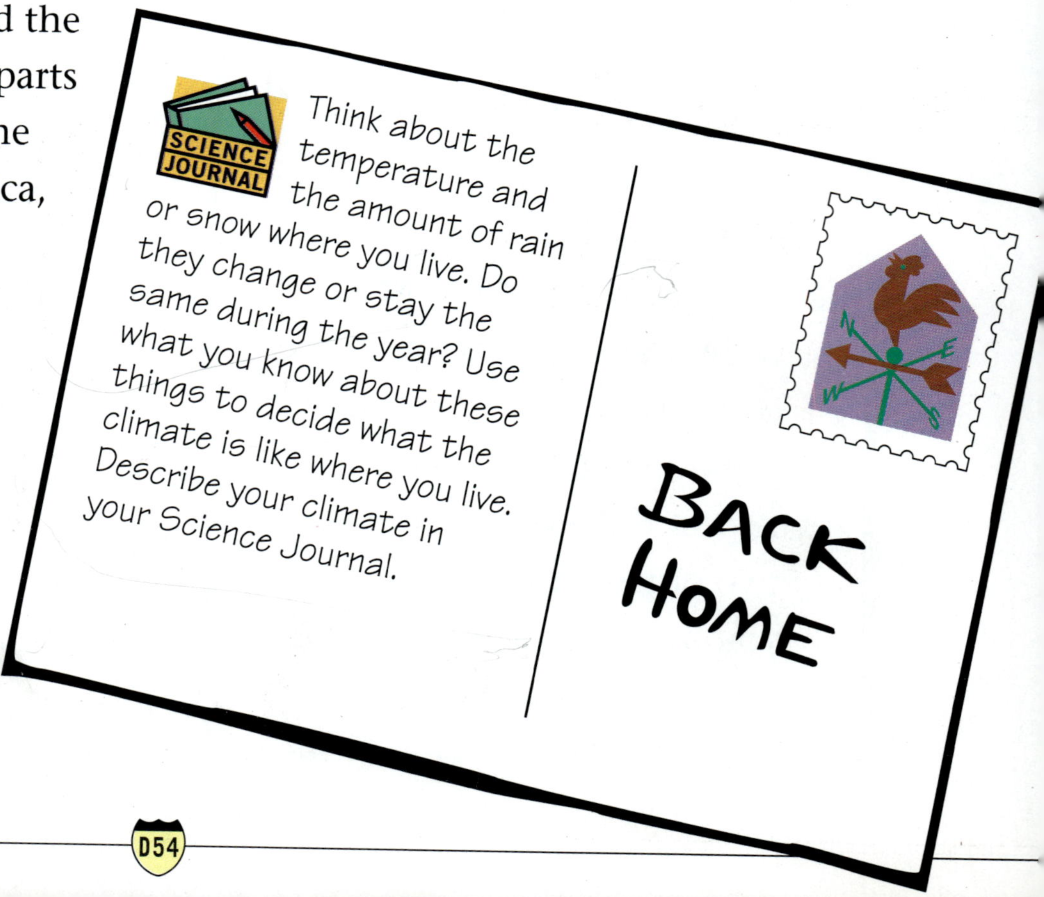

Here is the Danakil Desert in Ethiopia. This part of Ethiopia is very dry and covered with hardened lava. The white crusty patches you see are salt.

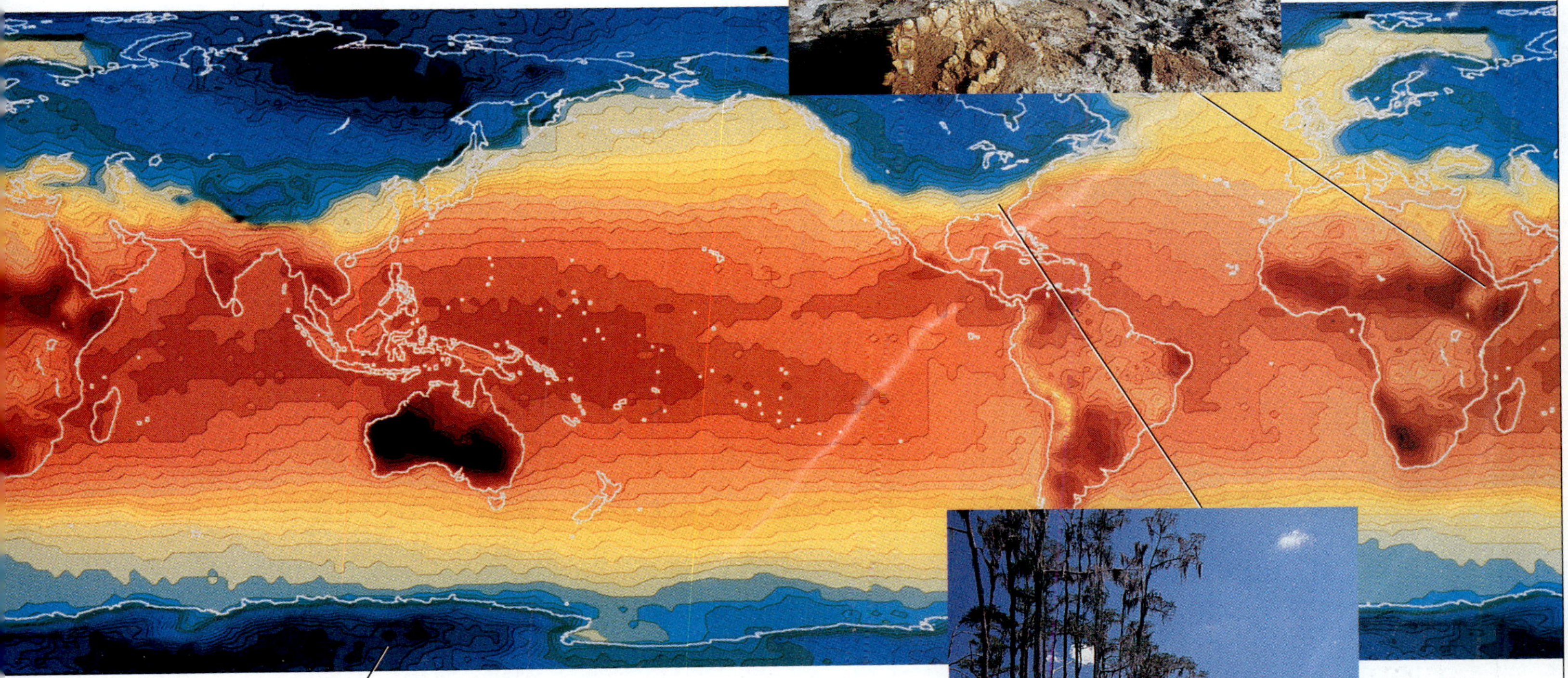

It is very cold in Antarctica. But these Adelie penguins don't mind the cold!

This is the Okefenokee Swamp, where the temperature doesn't change very much during the year.

How do people cause changes in climate?

Scientists believe that the world's climates have changed many times. They think these changes have had natural causes. Scientists also believe that people cause changes in climates.

When we burn fuels to get energy, we send carbon dioxide into the air. Too much carbon dioxide traps heat and holds it close to the earth's surface. Trapped heat may cause temperatures around the world to rise. This climate change is known as global warming.

Scientists wonder what the earth will be like if it continues to warm up. They don't really know the answer. Most scientists agree that people affect the world's climates. We must decrease the amount of carbon dioxide we are putting into the air. How could you help to prevent global warming?

When we burn fuel to run our cars, we put carbon dioxide into the air.

Global Warming

We burn fuels to get energy for many things, including heat and electricity. The gases produced from the burning of fuels trap heat close to the earth's surface. Are there any ways that you can help keep this from happening?

Think About It Imagine that you are asked to design a "fuel wise" building. Would it be easier to build "fuel wise" homes, schools, or businesses? Diagram or draw the building you think would use the least amount of fuel.

You don't need to ride in a car to go from one place to another. In New York City, many people ride a ferry boat to Staten Island instead of driving over in a car.

How are you doing?

1. What is climate?
2. What causes global warming?
3. **Think** What might happen if the world's climates got warmer?

Looking Back

Words and Concepts

Match the descriptions in Column A with the terms in Column B.

Column A

1. A place's weather over a long time
2. Spinning cloud with a funnel shape
3. One cause of global warming
4. Most common type of storm
5. Not enough rain for a long time
6. Large powerful kind of storm

Column B

a. Thunderstorm
b. Climate
c. Drought
d. Hurricane
e. Carbon dioxide
f. Tornado

Applied Thinking Skills

Answer the following questions. You can use words, drawings, and diagrams in your answers.

7. Why do floods often happen during hurricanes?
8. Why don't hurricanes form along the coast of Antarctica?
9. Why do you think a tornado might be more dangerous than a thunderstorm?
10. **Your World** How does mowing a lawn with a fuel-powered mower add to global warming?

Show What You Know

HANDS-ON ASSESSMENT

What kind of storm is it?

Observe and Collect Data

1. Look back in this chapter for four examples of different storms or weather conditions. Draw a picture of each storm or weather condition on an index card.
2. Divide a sheet of paper into four squares. Place one card in each square. Tape the left side of each card so it can be flipped over.
3. On the paper under each card, label and describe the type of storm or weather condition.

Process Skills

Inferring, Interpreting data

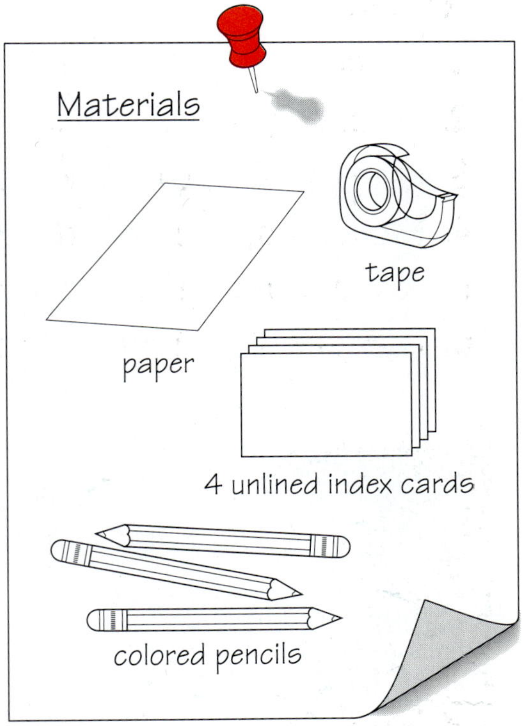

Draw Conclusions

1. Which storm or weather condition was the hardest to draw? Why?
2. Which one do you think can cause the most damage? Explain your answer.

Water & Weather

Show what you know about weather. Work by yourself, with a partner, or in a group.

Disaster Reporter How would you prepare for a storm at school? Write instructions you and your classmates would need to follow if a storm was coming. Read these instructions to the class and post them where everyone can see them.

Weather Wonderer Create a survey to find out what kind of weather people like and why. Include your classmates in the survey and present a chart of your findings to your class.

Cloud Artist Have you ever looked up into the sky and seen clouds that look like animals? Go outside on a cloudy day and look up. Draw or paint the pictures you see in the clouds. Label your art with the real names of the clouds.

Weather Musician Choose pieces of music that make you think of weather or the water cycle. Use them to help you create your own musical piece. Then play it for your classmates and explain how the weather or water cycle is connected to the music.

Weather Traveler You are going away on vacation. Pretend to pack a suitcase. Describe to the class what clothes and objects you are taking. Can your classmates guess what kind of climate you are traveling to?

Silent Weather Person Form a small group and decide how your group will pantomime a weather condition, such as a tornado or a sunny day. See if the class can guess what weather you are showing.

Glossary

anemometer (an′ə mäm′ət ər) An instrument that measures wind speed. (page D34)

cirrus cloud (sir′əs kloud) A cloud that is high in the sky and made of ice crystals. (page D39)

climate (klī′mət) The weather conditions of a place over time. (page D54)

condensation (kän′dən sā′shən) The change from water vapor to water. (page D14)

cumulonimbus cloud (kyo͞o′myo͞o lō nim′bəs kloud) A tall, dark cloud that produces thunderstorms. (page D39)

cumulus cloud (kyo͞o′myo͞o ləs kloud) Puffy cloud that usually occurs in sunny weather. (page D38)

evaporation (ē vap′ə rā′shən) The change from water to water vapor. (page D12)

fog (fôg) A cloud that forms at the earth's surface. (page D39)

ground water (ground wôt′ər) Fresh water that is found underground. (page D10)

humidity (hyo͞o mid′ə tē) The amount of water vapor in the air. (page D12)

meteorologist (mēt′ē ər äl′ə jist) A scientist who studies weather. (page D6)

stratus cloud (strāt′əs kloud) Gray clouds that drop rain or snow. (page D38)

weather (we*th*′ər) The condition of the air. (page D24)

wind vane (wind vān) An instrument that shows wind direction. (page D34)

Unit D Index

Boldface numerals denote glossary terms. Italic numerals denote illustrations.

Credits

Photographs

1 Warren Faidley/International Stock; 2–3 Anne Dowie*; 2CL Anne Dowie*; 2TL David Jeffrey/The Image Bank; 3 Anne Dowie*; 4BL Don & Pat Valenti/DRK Photo; 4BR Runk-Schoenberger/Grant Heilman Photography; 4CL Tom Tracy/The Stock Market; 4TR Art Wolfe/AllStock; 5 Ken Karp*; 6 Martin Dohrn/SPL/Photo Researchers; 7BL GHP Studio*; 7BR GHP Studio*; 7TL Mark Adams/Westlight; 7TR Phototheque Mon Tresor/Panoramic Images; 9 Ken Karp*; 10 Jose Azel/Woodfin Camp & Associates; 11 Peter Fronk/Tony Stone Images; 13BL David Muench/AllStock; 13BR Greg Probst/AllStock; 13T Chad Ehlers/Tony Stone Images; 14 Anne Dowie*; 15 David Sailors/The Stock Market; 17 Ken Karp*; 18 Stephen J. Krasemann/DRK Photo; 19 Ken Karp*; 23 Ken Karp*; 24–25 Ken Karp*; 24B John Lei/Stock, Boston; 25B Gerald L. French/Panoramic Images; 25T Bill Horsman/Stock, Boston; 26 Ken Karp*; 27 Ken Karp*; 28–29 Ken Karp*; 28T Warren Faidley/International Stock Photo; 29T Ken Karp*; 30 Erich Lessing/Art Resource; 31B Carla Breeze/Fundamental Photographs; 31T NASA/Science Source/Photo Researchers; 33 M. H. Black/Weatherstock; 34 Tim Davis*; 35L GHP Studio*; 35R Anne Dowie*; 36–37 Len Rue, Jr./Earth Scenes; 37R Liz Hymans/AllStock; 40B John Coletti/Stock, Boston; 40TC Ken Karp*; 40TL John Coletti/Stock, Boston; 41L Lawrence Migdale/Stock, Boston; 41R Ruth Dixon/Stock, Boston; 42 Richard Pasley/Stock, Boston; 43 Ken Karp*; 44–45 GHP Studio*; 46 John Bova/Photo Researchers; 47L David Epperson/AllStock; 47R Craig Aurness/Woodfin Camp & Associates; 48–49 Warren Faidley/International Stock Photo; 50B Steve Starr/Stock, Boston; 50T A. & J. Verkaik/The Stock Market; 51C Anne Dowie*; 51L Anne Dowie*; 51R Michael Holford; 52 Stewart D. Halperin/Earth Scenes; 53 Joe Jacobson/Panoramic Stock Images; 55BL George Holton/Photo Researchers; 55BR Jack Gardner/Stock South; 55T Volkman Wentzel/National Geographic Society; 55C NASA/Science Source/Photo Researchers; 56 Stephen Kline/Bruce Coleman Inc.; 57 Alan Pitcairn/Grant Heilman Photography; 58 Keith Brewster/Weatherstock; 59 Ken Karp*

*Photographed expressly for Addison-Wesley Publishing Company, Inc.

Illustrations

Nea Bisek 8T, 23, 26L, 41, 43, 59
Dave Carlson 22, 32, 35, 37
Shelton Leong 60–61
Jane McCreary 8B, 12, 27, 47
Laurie O'Keefe 28, 29
Precision Graphics 19, 26R, 49
Rosalind Solomon 38–39
Sarah Woodward 10, 12, 14, 16–17

Text

1 William Brighty Rands, "Topsy Turvey."

20–21 Mary Stolz, *Storm in the Night.* (New York: HarperCollins Publishers, 1988.) Text copyright © 1988 by Mary Stolz. Illustrations copyright © 1988 by Pat Cummings. Reprinted by permission of HarperCollins Publishers.

24 Weather Across the USA. Copyright, USA TODAY. Reprinted by permission.

59 Aquatic Project Wild, 1987.

Captain Hydro, East Bay Municipal Utility District, 1982.

50 Simple Things You Can Do to Save the Earth, The Earth Works Group, Earthworks Press, 1989.